HEALING THE GRIEVING HEART

Also by Alan Wolfelt:

A Child's View of Grief

Creating Meaningful Funeral Ceremonies:
A Guide for Caregivers

Healing the Bereaved Child:
Grief Gardening,
Growth Through Grief and
Other Touchstones for Caregivers

The Journey Through Grief:
Reflections on Healing

Understanding Grief: Helping Yourself Heal

*Companion Press is dedicated to the education
and support of both the bereaved and bereavement caregivers.*

*We believe that those who companion the bereaved
by walking with them as they journey in grief
have a wondrous opportunity: to help others embrace
and grow through grief—and to lead fuller,
more deeply-lived lives themselves
because of this important work.*

Companion
P R E S S

For a complete catalog
and ordering information,
write or call:

Companion Press
The Center for Loss and
Life Transition
3735 Broken Bow Road
Fort Collins, CO 80526
(970) 226-6050

HEALING THE GRIEVING HEART

100 PRACTICAL IDEAS FOR FAMILIES, FRIENDS AND CAREGIVERS

Alan D. Wolfelt, Ph.D.

Companion
PRESS

Fort Collins,
Colorado

An imprint of the
Center for Loss and
Life Transition

Companion Press is an imprint of the
Center for Loss and Life Transition,
3735 Broken Bow Road, Fort Collins, Colorado 80526.

Printed in the United States of America

07 06 05 04 03 02 01 00 99   5 4 3 2

ISBN: 1-879651-13-0

Publisher's Cataloging-in-Publication
(Provided by Quality Books, Inc.)

Wolfelt, Alan.
    Healing the grieving heart : 100 practical
ideas for families, friends & caregivers / Alan D.
Wolfelt. -- 1st ed.
    p. cm.
    ISBN: 1-879651-13-0

    1. Grief.   2. Bereavement --Psychological
aspects. 3. Loss (Psychology)   I. Title

BF575.G7W64 1999   155.9'37
                                     QBI99-539

In memory of Ben Allen.

*"Caring for another, we sometimes glimpse
an essential quality of our being…
We're reminded of who we really are and what
we have to offer one another."*

Ram Dass

Who found the Tail?

   "I," said Pooh,

"At a quarter to two

   (Only it was a quarter to eleven really),

I found the Tail!"

INTRODUCTION

In A.A. Milne's beloved Winnie-the-Pooh, there is a story "In Which Eeyore Loses a Tail and Pooh Finds One." The ever-dour Eeyore is moping about when the always-affable Pooh approaches and asks, "And how are you?"

"Not very how," Eeyore replies. "I don't seem to have felt at all how for a long time."

It turns out that Eeyore's tail is missing.

The story continues:

> Pooh felt that he ought to say something helpful about it, but didn't quite know what. So he decided to *do* something helpful instead.
>
> "Eeyore," he said solemnly, "I, Winnie-the-Pooh, will find your tail for you."
>
> "Thank you, Pooh," answered Eeyore. "You're a real friend."

The purpose of this book is to help you "do something helpful" for a grieving friend. To be bereaved is to be "torn apart" and to "have special needs." Your friend probably isn't feeling very "how" these days, either. Like Pooh, you may not always know what to say (see Ideas 11-15 for tips on listening and verbal support). But you can *do* many helpful, supportive, loving things to help your friend through her unique grief journey. For some time now I have been teaching the concept of "companioning" in the many grief workshops I teach across North America each year. I have taken liberties with the noun "companion" and made it into the verb "companioning" because it so well captures the type of helping relationship between friend and mourner that I advocate. Actually, the word companion, when broken down into its original Latin roots means "messmate" or "with bread." Someone you would share a meal with. A friend.

Your friend needs a companion in grief right now. (A whole network of companions would be best, but let's isolate your role as companion in this discussion.) He needs someone who will be present to him, who will bear witness to his struggle, who will honor his unique journey through grief.

As promised, this book contains 100 practical ideas for friends, family members and caregivers who want to help mourners heal. Some of the ideas will teach you about the principles of grief and mourning. One of the most important ways you can help your friend is to learn about the grief experience; the more you know, the less likely you will be to unknowingly perpetuate some of our society's harmful myths about grief and healing.

The most fundamental principles of companioning a friend in grief are:

- Listening.

  Helping begins with your ability to be an active listener. Your physical presence and desire to listen without judging are critical helping tools. Don't worry so much about what you will say. Just concentrate on listening to the words that are being shared with you.

- Having compassion.

  Give your friend permission to express his feelings without fear of criticism. Learn from your friend; don't instruct or set expectations about how he should respond. Never say, "I know just how you feel." You don't. Think about your helper role as someone who "walks with," not behind or in front of the one who is mourning.

- Understanding the uniqueness of grief.

  Keep in mind that your friend's grief is unique. While it may be possible to talk about similar "phases" shared by grieving people, everyone is different and shaped by experiences in their own unique lives. Because the grief experience is also unique, be patient. The process of grief takes a long time, so allow your friend to proceed at her own pace.

- Being there.

  Your ongoing and reliable presence is the most important gift you can give your grieving friend. While you cannot take the pain away (nor should you try to), you can enter into it through being there for him. Remain available in the weeks, months and years to come. Remember that your friend may need you more later on than at the time of the death.

The remainder of the 100 ideas offer practical, here-and-now, action-oriented tips for companioning your mourning friend. Each idea is followed by a brief explanation of how and why the idea might help your friend.

You'll also notice that each of the 100 ideas suggests a *carpe diem*, which means, as fans of the movie *Dead Poets Society* will remember, "seize the day." My hope is that you will not relegate this book to your shelves but keep it handy on your nightstand or desk. Pick it up often and turn to any page; the *carpe diem* suggestion will help you seize the day by supporting your friend today, right now, right this minute. If you come to an idea that doesn't seem to fit your friend, ignore it and flip to a different page.

Being a real friend to someone during this extraordinarily difficult time won't be easy. It may test your patience, your character, your fortitude—and your deepest reserves of compassion. But I promise you that if you commit to being present to a friend in grief, to companioning him through what may well be his darkest hours, you will be rewarded with the deep satisfaction of having helped a fellow human being heal.

I challenge you to take action by being there for your friend and offering your unwavering companionship. I challenge you to find Eeyore's tail. I challenge you to be a real friend in grief.

Sincerely,

Alan D. Wolfelt

UNDERSTAND THE DIFFERENCE BETWEEN GRIEF AND MOURNING.

- Grief is the constellation of internal thoughts and feelings we have when someone loved dies.

- Mourning is the outward expression of our grief.

- Everyone who has the capacity to give and receive love grieves when someone loved dies, but if we are to heal, we must also mourn.

- You can help by creating "safe places" for your friend to mourn in ways that fit her personality. If she would like to talk, encourage her to talk. If she likes to write, encourage her to keep a journal. The key is to find forms of expression that are appropriate for the individual. There is no one "right" way to mourn.

CARPE DIEM:
Consider the past losses in your own life. Did you mourn those deaths? If not, what were the consequences of repressing your thoughts and feelings?

2

CARPE DIEM:
You may sense
circumstances
surrounding the
death that your
friend needs to talk
about over and over
again. Commit your-
self to gently explore
these with your
friend. Your task is
not to have answers,
but to listen with
your heart.

UNDERSTAND THE SIX NEEDS OF MOURNING.

Need #1: Acknowledge the reality of the death.

- Your friend must confront the reality that someone he
  loved is dead and will never physically be present to him
  again.

- Whether the death was sudden or anticipated,
  acknowledging the full reality of the loss may occur over
  weeks and months.

- At times your friend may, in his heart or aloud, push away
  some of the reality of the death. This is normal. He will
  come to embrace the reality in doses as he is ready.

- When your friend expresses his thoughts about the fact of
  the death, he is working on this important need. You can
  help by listening.

UNDERSTAND THE SIX
NEEDS OF MOURNING.

Need #2: Embrace the pain of the loss.

- This need requires mourners to embrace the pain of their loss—something they naturally don't want to do. It is easier to avoid, repress or deny the pain of grief than it is to confront it.

- It is in confronting her grief, however, that your friend will learn to reconcile herself to it.

- Your friend will probably need to "dose" herself in embracing her pain. If she were to allow in all the pain at once, she would be overwhelmed.

- Don't buy into the myth that if your friend seems to be experiencing little pain, she is "doing well" with her grief.

CARPE DIEM:
Symbols of support often bring comfort to people experiencing the pain of grief. Think of a symbol you can take to your friend this week that will provide a balm for the pain. Consider flowers, comfort food, a hope-filled book.

4

UNDERSTAND THE SIX NEEDS OF MOURNING.

Need #3: Remember the person who died.

- When someone loved dies, they live on in us through memory.

- Your friend needs to actively remember the person who died and commemorate the life that was lived.

- Never try to take your friend's memories away in a misguided attempt to save him from pain. It's good for him to continue to display photos of the person who died. Realizing it is not always possible or appropriate, many mourners also find comfort in staying in the residence they shared with the person who died.

- Remembering the past makes hoping for the future possible.

CARPE DIEM:
Choose a special, appropriate frame to hold a photo of the person who died. Give it to your friend this week along with a note explaining what the frame is for and why you chose this particular one.

UNDERSTAND THE SIX NEEDS OF MOURNING.

Need #4: Develop a new self-identity

- Part of your friend's self-identity was formed by the relationship she had with the person who died.

- She may have gone from being a "wife" to a "widow" or from a "parent" to a "bereaved parent." The way she defined herself and the way society defined her is changed.

- Your friend needs to re-anchor herself, to reconstruct her self-identity. This is arduous and painful work.

- Many mourners discover that as they work on this need, they ultimately discover some positive changes, such as becoming more caring or less judgmental.

CARPE DIEM:
Write your friend a note that both honors her old identity and demonstrates allegiance to her new one. For example: "You and Bob had a marriage I admired. I want you to know that I continue to admire and respect you as the unique person you are."

6

UNDERSTAND THE SIX NEEDS OF MOURNING.

Need #5: Search for meaning.

- When someone loved dies, we naturally question the meaning and purpose of life and death.

- "Why?" questions may surface uncontrollably and often precede "How?" questions. "Why did this happen?" comes before "How will I go on living?"

- Your friend will probably question his philosophy of life and explore religious and spiritual values as he works on this need.

- Now is not the time to foist your own religious views on your friend.

CARPE DIEM:

When you hear your friend questioning the meaning of life and death, commit yourself to not thinking you have to have answers. Ask to sit beside him instead of across from him as he explores the "whys."

UNDERSTAND THE SIX NEEDS OF MOURNING.

Need #6: Receive ongoing support from others.

- Mourners need the love and understanding of others if they are to heal.

- By helping a friend in grief, you are helping her meet this need of mourning.

- Unfortunately, our society places too much value on "carrying on" and "doing well" after a death. So, many mourners are abandoned by their friends and family soon after the death.

- Grief is a process, not an event, and your friend will need your continued support for weeks, months and years.

CARPE DIEM:
Stop for a moment and think: When did your friend's loved one die? Has your support for her waned since the funeral? Has your contact been less and less frequent? Commit right now to contacting or spending time with your friend every week this year.

8

MAKE A "CONTACT PACT" WITH YOURSELF.

- Commit to contacting your friend once a week/month.

- Vary your means and time of contact so your friend won't feel he's just an item on your "to do" list.

- Your contact needn't take a lot of time; a brief phone call or a short note are enough to demonstrate your support.

- Don't neglect your friend as time passes; mourners need support long after the event of the death.

CARPE DIEM:
Right now, pick up your appointment book and schedule a regular, ongoing time to contact your friend. Write it down!

ATTEND THE FUNERAL.

- Funerals are our way of saying goodbye to the person who died and honoring the life that was lived. They are also our way of demonstrating our support for those most impacted by the death.

- Even if you didn't personally know the person who died, it's appropriate for you to attend the funeral to show your support for your friend.

- Try hard to attend all the phases of the funeral—the visitation, the funeral, the committal and the gathering afterwards.

CARPE DIEM:
If the funeral was meaningful to you, let your friend know. Many mourners feel comforted by the knowledge that it was a "good funeral."

10

CARPE DIEM:
If appropriate, assemble a funeral "scrapbook" for your friend. Include the obituary from the newspaper, the program from the funeral ceremony and leave plenty of room for your friend to insert sympathy cards and other mementos.

RECORD THE FUNERAL FOR POSTERITY.

- It's common for mourners to feel numb in the first days and weeks following the death. Often the funeral feels like a blur.

- Later, though, many mourners find comfort in the memory of the funeral. "I wish I could remember just what Pastor Johnson said," they think.

- Arrange for the funeral home to have the funeral ceremony videotaped or audiotaped. Then, when you think she's ready, offer to sit down and view or listen to the tape with her.

- Still photography is usually considered taboo at funerals, though people of some cultures photograph the dead as a way of capturing and honoring the end of a person's life.

LISTEN WITHOUT JUDGING.

- The most important gift you can give your grieving friend is the gift of your presence. Be there for him. Initiate contact. And listen, listen, listen.

- Listen some more. If he wants to talk about the death over and over again, listen patiently each time. Telling and retelling the story helps mourners heal.

- Don't worry so much about what you will say in return; instead, concentrate on the words being shared with you.

CARPE DIEM:
Commit yourself right now to visiting your friend within the next 72 hours. Promise yourself that you will focus on being the best possible listener. Keep in mind the 80/20 ratio: your friend should talk 80% of the time to your 20%!

12

CARPE DIEM:
If you feel like you just can't listen to your friend's pain right now, make an effort to stay in contact through letters, short phone calls, token gifts of your support. Perhaps in a month or so you'll feel more able to listen to her thoughts and feelings.

UNDERSTAND WHY LISTENING CAN BE DIFFICULT.

• Sometimes listening to a friend in grief talk about her thoughts and feelings or recount the story of the death can be uncomfortable for us as friends.

• Listening may stimulate unreconciled grief in us and demand exploration of pain and trauma.

• Listening to others struggle can also leave us feeling helpless and ineffectual.

• It is through being aware of our helplessness that we ultimately become helpful. Worry if you always think you know what to say. Remember—mouth closed, ears open. Just your quiet presence will be helpful.

DON'T FALL BACK ON CLICHÉS.

- Mourners' deep and extremely complicated feelings of loss are often dismissed with overly simple, empty phrases such as:

  - Give it time.
  - Keep busy.
  - Be strong.
  - At least he didn't suffer.
  - It's time to move on.
  - He lived a long life.
  - Try not to think about it.

  - You'll become stronger because of this.
  - Be glad you had him as long as you did.
  - He wouldn't have wanted you to be sad.
  - Life is for the living.

- Though well-intended, such clichés hurt because they diminish the mourner's feelings and take away his right to mourn.

CARPE DIEM:
Read Idea 15 right now. That way you'll be better equipped to talk to your friend next time you meet.

14

CARPE DIEM:
If you've used any of the phrases on this page or the page before, don't worry too much. Your friend knows you were trying to help. But make an effort from this day forward not to fall back on clichés again as you attempt to help a friend in grief.

DON'T USE RELIGIOUS CLICHÉS, EITHER:

- Sometimes people use theologized clichés in an attempt to comfort:
    - It was God's will.
    - God only gives you what you can handle.
    - Now she's in a better place.
    - This is a blessing.
    - Now you have an angel in heaven.

- Like other clichés, these expressions tend to minimize the mourner's loss.
- Your friend may have faith but still needs to mourn this death.

DO SAY THIS:

- I'm sorry.
- I'm thinking of you.
- I care.
- I love you.
- You are so important to me.
- I'm here for you.
- I want to help.
- I'm thinking of you and praying for you every day.
- I want you to know I loved _____.

CARPE DIEM:
Call your friend tomorrow morning and say, "I just want you to know I'm thinking of you."

16

EXPECT YOUR FRIEND TO HAVE A MULTITUDE OF FEELINGS.

- Mourners don't just feel sad. They may feel numb, angry, guilty, afraid, confused or even relieved. Sometimes these feelings follow each other within a short period of time or they may occur simultaneously.

- As strange as some of these emotions may seem to you, they are normal and healthy.

- Allow your friend to express whatever she's feeling without judgment. Your job is to listen, listen, listen.

- Enter into what she thinks and feels without thinking you have to change what she thinks and feels.

CARPE DIEM:
Try this "active listening" technique with your friend. The next time she shares her feelings with you, summarize by saying, "So you're feeling _____ because _____."

ALLOW YOUR FRIEND TO CRY.

17

- Tears are a natural cleansing and healing mechanism. It's OK to cry. In fact, it's good to cry when you feel like it. Plus, tears are a form of mourning. They are sacred!

- Most people are uncomfortable when others cry in their presence. For the sake of your friend, try not to be one of those people.

- If your friend cries when you're with her, resist the urge to hand her a Kleenex or hug her right away. Though loving and well-intended, both of these responses tend to send the message that you'd like her to stop crying.

- Instead, lean into her and simply be present. Of course, if you sense that she wants your touch, by all means hold her hand or give her a hug.

CARPE DIEM:
If your friend has been crying a lot, write her a brief note that says you're sorry she's hurting right now but that you understand her need to cry—and that she can cry in your presence whenever she wants to.

18

CARPE DIEM:
Purchase a gift
certificate for your
friend to get a
massage. Include a
supportive note and
mail it or drop it off
today.

REACH OUT AND TOUCH.

- For many people, physical contact with another human
  being is healing. It has been recognized since ancient times
  as having transformative, healing powers.

- Have you hugged your mourning friend lately? Held his
  hand? Put your arm around him?

- Consider hugging your friend every time you see him.
  This little ritual will convey how much you care more than
  words ever could.

- Pay attention to body language. If your friend stiffens or
  moves away when you touch, don't continue. Not everyone
  is a hugger.

BE AWARE THAT YOUR FRIEND'S GRIEF AFFECTS HER BODY, HEART, SOCIAL SELF AND SPIRIT.

19

- Grief is physically demanding. The body responds to the stress of the encounter and the immune system can weaken. Mourners are more susceptible to illness and physical discomforts. They also often feel highly fatigued.

- The emotional toll of grief is complex and painful. Mourners often feel many different feelings, and those feelings can shift and blur over time.

- Bereavement naturally results in social discomfort. Friends and family often withdraw from mourners, leaving them isolated and unsupported.

- Mourners often ask themselves: Why go on living? Will my life have meaning now? Where is God in this? Spiritual questions are natural and necessary but also draining.

CARPE DIEM:
Has your friend felt well lately? Has she told you she's really tired or has had headaches? Understand that her physical ailments may be a result of her grief and deserve your compassionate support just as much as her emotional pain.

20

USE THE NAME OF THE PERSON WHO DIED.

- When you're talking to your mourning friend, don't avoid using the name of the person who died. Avoiding it diminishes the loss.

- Instead, acknowledge the significance of the death by talking about the person who died: "I remember when David …", "When did you and Anne meet?", "I thought of Julie today because … "

- Using the name of the person who died personalizes your concern and expresses your willingness to honor "telling the story."

CARPE DIEM:
When you talk to your friend today, share a memory of the person who died. Use his or her name.

WRITE A LETTER.

- A sympathy note, when written with genuineness and compassion, can be very comforting for mourners.

- Communicate your concern and support, but avoid clichés.

- Share memories of the person who died if appropriate.

- Send your letter at a time when other support is waning— weeks or even months after the death.

CARPE DIEM:
Pick up a blank card and begin your note with this phrase: *I'm so sorry that . . .*
Write from the heart.

22

CARPE DIEM:
Bring a bunch of
seasonal flowers to
your friend. In
the spring, pick a
bouquet of violets or
cut branches of
forsythia from your
own yard. Potted
poinsettia or amaryl-
lis are thoughtful at
Christmas time.

SAY IT WITH FLOWERS.

- Flowers symbolize love and beauty and say for us
  what we could not possibly say at a time when words are
  inadequate.

- The current "in lieu of flowers" trend denigrates the power
  of this traditional gift.

- Sending flowers in the weeks and months after the death is
  a nice way to show your ongoing support.

- Alternatives to cut flowers include potted plants, hanging
  baskets, bulbs, tree seedlings and planted perennials at the
  grave site.

SERVE AS "SOCIAL NETWORK ADMINISTRATOR."

- Many people don't now how to help their mourning friend.

- You can galvanize the mourner's network of friends and family by phoning them and helping individuals choose a way to help.

- Say, "Joe is really going to need help this year. I was just wondering if…

    … you could check on him once a week."

    … you could help him with groceries and meals. I hear you're a great cook."

    … you'd given any thought to how you could help."

- Be firm and specific without being confrontive.

CARPE DIEM:
Contact one or two of your friend's neighbors and ask them to help keep an eye on your friend's house, yard, pets, etc. Most are more than happy to help when asked.

24

CARPE DIEM:
Phone a local deli and ask them to assemble a dinner basket. Drop it off at your friend's house tonight. Take a single rose (or a flower you know your friend likes) and let her know the flower is in memory of _____ (the person who died).

PLAY CATERER FOR AN EVENING.

- Food represents love and nurturance.
- Bring her a favorite meal—appetizers to dessert.
- Also consider favorite foods of the person who died.
- Copy down a blessing to be read before the meal—or write your own!
- If it feels right, stay and share your supportive presence.

OFFER BEVERAGES, TOO.

- Grief sometimes overrides the mourner's thirst mechanism.

- Dehydration can compound feelings of fatigue and disorientation.

- Gently remind your friend to drink 4-5 glasses of water each day.

- Put together a gift basket with your friend's favorite non-alcoholic, non-caffeinated drinks—teas, sparkling waters, hot chocolate, etc.

CARPE DIEM:
Buy your friend a gift certificate to a local juice bar. Write a "thinking of you" card and enclose the certificate. Mail it today!

26

DON'T EXPECT YOUR FRIEND TO MOURN OR HEAL IN A CERTAIN WAY OR IN A CERTAIN TIME.

CARPE DIEM:
Next time you're with your friend, remember to use the "teach me" principle of learning about his grief. If you listen, he will likely teach you about the various influences listed at right.

- Your friend's unique grief journey will be shaped by many factors, including:
  - the nature of the relationship he had with the person who died.
  - the age of the person who died.
  - the circumstances of the death.
  - his unique personality.
  - his cultural background.
  - his religious or spiritual beliefs.
  - his gender.
  - his support systems.

- Because of these and other factors, no two deaths are ever mourned in precisely the same way.

- Don't have rigid expectations for your friend's thoughts, feelings and behaviors. Instead, think of your role as one who "walks with," not behind or in front of your friend.

BE HER HANDYPERSON.

- Daily chores and home maintenance can be overwhelming for mourners.

- Tasks that used to be taken care of by the person who died can be especially difficult.

- Take a look around her home and do whatever needs doing—washing dishes, raking leaves, changing lightbulbs, caring for pets.

- Don't ask, just do—but take care not to offend or shame her or other household members.

CARPE DIEM:
Consider the season. Spring? Stop by and wash your friend's windows. Summer? Cut the grass. Fall? Rake leaves. Winter? Change the furnace filter.

28

BE HIS ERRAND BOY/GIRL.

- As with home chores, necessary errands can be overwhelming for mourners.

- Be especially aware of any barriers your friend has to completing tasks or doing errands himself (can't drive, has small children, too depressed).

- Grocery shop, pick up kids from soccer, buy stamps, etc.

- Go yourself or offer to drive and help your friend.

CARPE DIEM:
Call your friend and ask what you can pick up for him at the store today.

TAKE YOUR FRIEND TO THE MOVIES.

- Movies tend to be healing, even for less emotional mourners.

- Pick a movie about loss if you think it will help spur needed discussion.

- Choose a comedy if your friend needs a pick-me-up.

- Plays can also be moving; check local theater groups' schedules.

- Afterwards, stop for pie and coffee.

CARPE DIEM:
Drop by your friend's house this evening with a rented movie and take-out food. Call first if she's not the spontaneous type.

30

GO BUY THE BOOK.

- You'll find many good books on mourning and grief at local bookstores and libraries.

- Workbooks (journals, written exercises) can be especially helpful.

- Poetry, religious texts, even novels about loss may be appropriate for some.

- A warning: new mourners may not be ready for so much information or introspection.

CARPE DIEM:
Call Companion Press (970/226-6050) and order your friend a copy of *Healing Your Grieving Heart: 100 Practical Ideas,* which is the companion book to this one.

BE MINDFUL OF ANNIVERSARIES.

- Anniversaries—of the death, life events, birthdays—can be especially difficult for mourners.

- Call your friend and offer your support.

- Be direct; say, "I know Bill died six months ago today and I was thinking about you." Let your friend take the lead from there.

- Planning an anniversary date activity in advance might be a welcome invitation for some mourners.

CARPE DIEM:
Write down the anniversary of the death as well as the birthdays of the person who died and your friend in your appointment book. That way you won't forget the days that may be hardest for your friend.

32

PLANT SEEDS OF HOPE.

- Gardening represents growth, beauty, natural cycles of life and death.

- Indoors or out, gardening is often healing for mourners.

- If your friend already gardens, encourage her by bringing seeds or seedlings, helping prepare the soil, pulling weeds, etc.

- Non-gardeners might start with a container garden or an indoor plant.

CARPE DIEM:
Take a cutting from your garden. Once it's rooted and planted in a pot, bring it to your friend. Write a note describing the plant and its care.

HELP HER TAKE CARE OF HERSELF.

- Good self-care is nurturing and necessary for mourners, yet it's something most completely overlook.

- Remind your friend about scheduling routine medical and dental checks.

- Ask her how much sleep she's been getting. Buy her a good new pillow.

- Gift certificates for day spas, massages, facials, haircuts, etc. are welcome gifts.

CARPE DIEM:
Treat your friend with a "do-it-your-self spa" kit. Fill a basket with plush towels in colorful hues, rich bath soaps, sea sponges, candles and a good book. Include a note of support and encouragement.

ACCOMPANY YOUR FRIEND TO THE CEMETERY.

- Some mourners appreciate having someone to talk to during cemetery visits.

- Ask your friend why this cemetery was chosen. Her answer may help her articulate some of her feelings about death and the person who died.

- Allow your friend some private time at the grave while you return to the car or go for a walk.

- Memorial Day, Veteran's Day, Labor Day, Mother's Day or Father's Day are traditional days to visit the cemetery and pay respects.

- If the body was cremated, visit the scattering site or columbarium with your friend.

CARPE DIEM:
Offer to help your friend plant flowers or bulbs at the grave site.

DIG OUT YOUR PARCHEESI BOARD.

- Board and card games are a simple, non-touchy-feely way to offer your supportive presence to less social or less talkative mourners.

- Doing jigsaw puzzles with your friend can provide a sense of a shared and ongoing goal.

- If your friend enjoys the game, offer to play once a week or once a month.

- Some mourners would enjoy participating in a game group—bridge club, bingo, poker.

CARPE DIEM:
Wrap up a board game as a gift for your friend then drop by and suggest a quick game.

36

When your friend
is ready, offer to help
him sort through the
personal effects of
the person who
died. Help create a
memory box filled
with significant
objects and memen-
tos. If he's not ready
to get rid of the
remainder of the
objects, that's OK.

UNDERSTAND THE ROLE OF "LINKING OBJECTS."

- Many mourners are comforted by physical objects
  associated with the person who died. It is not unusual for
  mourners to save clothing, jewelry, toys, locks of hair and
  other personal items.

- Such "linking objects" may help your friend remember the
  person who died and honor the life that was lived. Such
  objects may help your friend heal.

- Never suggest that being attached to these objects is
  morbid or wrong.

- Never hurry your friend into disposing of the personal
  effects of the person who died. Many mourners want to
  leave the personal items untouched for many years. This is
  OK as long as the objects offer comfort and don't inhibit
  healing.

BE A SPORT.

- Some mourners appreciate the social contact and camaraderie of participating in or watching sports.

- Ascertain your friend's interests then extend an invitation to play golf, handball, shoot hoops, watch football, attend a baseball game, etc.

- Play regularly if your friend would like.

- Male mourners are often very receptive to venting their feelings on the playing field.

CARPE DIEM:
What sport do you enjoy? Invite your friend to try it with you sometime this week.

38

JOIN THE CLUB.

- Many mourners would benefit from regular participation in a social organization because they provide friendship, routine, plans for the future.

- Book discussion groups, Kiwanis, singing groups, environmental organizations—you know your friend; help her find a group she'd enjoy.

- Political groups and human service organizations (Sierra Club, United Way, etc.) can provide purpose, satisfaction.

- If your friend is hesitant, offer to join, too, or connect her with a "sponsor" from the group.

CARPE DIEM:
Check your local paper for a listing of club and organization meetings. Clip the list and mail it to your friend along with a supportive note from you.

DON'T TALK ABOUT YOUR OWN LOSSES, AT LEAST NOT EARLY IN YOUR FRIEND'S GRIEF.

- Let this loss be the unique loss it is. Resist the urge to share your own grief stories early in your friend's grief journey.

- If your friend asks how you felt about a death in your life, by all means answer him. But try to avoid monopolizing the conversation.

- Never compare losses. No two deaths are ever mourned precisely the same. Don't offer judgments about which loss was worse.

CARPE DIEM:
Write down the following definition of the helping concept of immediacy: "to be present to my friend in ways that keep the focus on him or her." Place this definition somewhere you will see it often.

40

TAKE A DRIVE.

- Out of the blue one day, invite your friend on a leisurely drive with you.

- A change of place and scenery can help ease depression and lend perspective.

- Confinement in a car may encourage conversation.

- Drive to a distant gourmet restaurant, nearby community or park—or no special destination.

CARPE DIEM:
Choose a scenic spot an hour or two away and ask your friend to drive there with you this weekend.

INVITE YOUR FRIEND TO YOUR HOME.

- Social invitations give mourners something to look forward to and can help combat depression.

- Plan a dinner party followed by a group game (e.g. Trivial Pursuit).

- An informal dinner with your family might be easier for some mourners.

- Don't take refusals personally; some mourners won't be ready for socializing.

CARPE DIEM:
Consider your friend's talents then invite her to your house to help or to teach you to make homemade pasta, plan a garden, build bookshelves, etc.

42

CARPE DIEM:
Stop by your
local bookstore
and choose an
appropriate journal
for your friend.
Have it gift-wrapped
and drop it off at
your friend's house
or mail it to him on
your way home.

GIVE HIM A BLANK BOOK.

- Journals are an ideal way for some mourners to record their thoughts and feeling.

- Remember—inner thoughts and feelings of grief need to be expressed outwardly (including writing) if the mourner is to heal.

- If you'd like, begin the journal yourself by writing a supportive note to your friend.

ORGANIZE A TREE PLANTING.

- Trees represent the beauty, vibrancy and continuity of life.

- A specially planted and located tree honors the person who died and serves as a perennial memorial. Ask your friend where and when she might like a tree planted.

- You might write a short ceremony for the tree planting. Consider a personalized metal marker or sign, too.

- For a more private option, give a tree as a gift for your friend's own yard. Consult your local nursery for an appropriate selection, have it delivered and include a note about the tree's meaning.

CARPE DIEM:
Order a tree for your own yard and plant it in honor of the person who died. Share what you've done with your friend. This idea is especially appropriate if you, too, knew and cared about the person who died.

PLAN A WEEKLY WALK TOGETHER

- Exercise can be sustaining and invigorating for mourners.

- Walk every week at the same time; routines help mourners survive.

- Your walks might be a good time to talk about his grief or a time of supportive quiet.

- Other options: biking, swimming, gardening, health club visits—anything that gets you both moving. You know your friend; select options he'd like.

CARPE DIEM:
Invite your friend to accompany you on a mid-day walk—outside if the weather permits or indoors at your local mall.

GO WITH YOUR FRIEND TO A YOGA CLASS.

- Classes in yoga or other meditative activities can provide mourners with a structured format for spiritual time.

- The physical activity component is beneficial, too.

- Other options: tai chi, fly fishing, ballet.

- There are many excellent books about these and other activities that can help your friend get started with physical and spiritual self-care.

CARPE DIEM:
Purchase a gift certificate for your friend to an introductory yoga class.

46

CARPE DIEM:
If you were to
choose a "need of
mourning" that you
see your friend
working on right
now, which would it
be? Realizing your
friend's grief is not
orderly, is there a
particular need she
is teaching you that
is taking precedence?

KNOW THAT GRIEF DOES NOT PROCEED IN ORDERLY, PREDICTABLE "STAGES."

- Though the "Needs of Mourning" (Ideas 2-7) are numbered 1-6, grief is not an orderly progression towards healing. Don't fall into the trap of thinking your friend's grief journey will be predictable or always forward-moving.

- Usually, grief hurts more before it hurts less.

- Your friend will probably experience a multitude of different emotions in a wave-like fashion. She will also likely encounter more than one need of mourning at the same time.

PLAN A CEREMONY.

- When words are inadequate, have ceremony.

- Ceremony assists in reality, recall, support, expression, transcendence.

- The ceremony might center on memories of the person who died, "meaning of life" thoughts and feelings or affirmation of faith.

- Ceremony helps us know what to do when we do not know what to do.

CARPE DIEM:
Offer to hold a candle-lighting memory ceremony. With a small group of friends, form a circle. Each person holds and lights their own candle while sharing a memory of the person who died. At the end, read a poem or prayer in memory of the person who died.

48

CAPE DIEM:
Make today a
self-care day. Take
the day off from
thinking you have to
help your friend. Go
play. Do whatever it
is that renews you.

COUNT YOUR BLESSINGS.

- Helping a friend in grief can be extremely draining. It can also cause feelings of grief and fear for losses past and future to well up inside you.

- Are you worried that what happened to your friend might happen to you? If so, share those concerns with someone you trust. Refrain from sharing them with your mourning friend, however, because it may be perceived as selfish or petty.

- Take a deep breath and focus on enjoying the moment.

ORGANIZE A MEMORY BOOK.

- If the person who died was a member of your own social circle, it might be nice for you to surprise your friend with a memory book.

- Phone others who loved the person who died and ask them to write a note or contribute photos.

- Assemble the book and present it to your friend at an appropriate time. Honoring the first anniversary of the death with a memory book, for example, will let your friend know he's still very much in your thoughts.

- Other ideas: a memory box, photo buttons of the person who died (nice for a child or younger person), a memory quilt.

CARPE DIEM:
Focus on memories you share with your mourning friend for a minute. Write him a note relating two or three of these memories and remind him how much you care about him.

50

GET UP WITH THE BIRDS.

- The sun is a powerful symbol of life and renewal.

- When was the last time you watched the sun rise? Do you remember being touched by the beauty and power?

- Invite your friend for an early morning breakfast or walk in a location where you can see the sun rise. Hike to the top of a hill. Have coffee on a patio next to a lake.

- Sometimes mourners have trouble sleeping and may be up very early anyway. Your friend may appreciate sharing the dawn with you.

CARPE DIEM:
Invite your friend on an early morning drive. Choose a fitting destination for watching the sun rise. Pack a brunch of hot coffee, rolls, fresh fruit.

SUBSCRIBE TO FRIENDSHIP.

- There are a number of healing magazines for mourners. Most include mourner's stories of loss and renewed hope, poetry, meaningful artwork.

- One of this author's favorites is *Bereavement*, a bimonthly magazine filled with personal stories of loss and healing, grief education, poetry, etc. At the time of this writing, a one-year subscription within the U.S. costs $32 and can be ordered through the Center for Loss and Life Transition, (970) 226-6050.

- Instead of a grief magazine, consider giving your friend a gift subscription to a magazine you know she'd like, perhaps one on gardening or travel.

CARPE DIEM:
Call the number above and enter a gift subscription for your friend.

52

CARPE DIEM:
Invite your friend to
teach you about any
griefbursts he may
be having. It can be
reassuring to "talk
them out" and feel
affirmed that they
are normal. Or
buy him a journal
so he can note and
perhaps come to
understand his
griefbursts.

DON'T BE CAUGHT OFF GUARD BY "GRIEFBURSTS."

- Sometimes heightened periods of sadness will overwhelm your friend. These times can seem to come out of nowhere.

- Even long after the death, something as simple as a sound, a smell or a phrase can bring on a griefburst.

- You may feel helpless when your friend is feeling so low, but it is important for you to allow him to feel his sorrow.

THINK YOUNG.

- It is the nature of children to live for the moment and appreciate today. All of us would benefit from a little more childlike wonder.

- Do something childish with your friend—blow bubbles, skip rope, visit a toy store, build a sand castle, fly a kite, climb a tree.

- Make arrangements for your friend to spend time with kids if kids aren't already a part of her life. Invite her to visit the zoo with you and your children. Take her to a school play.

CARPE DIEM:
Buy an inexpensive gift for your friend at a local toy store— perhaps a paddle ball, a yo-yo, crayons. Wrap it in colorful paper and drop it off to your friend.

PET A PET.

- Pets are a comforting, loving part of many people's lives. Their physical presence and unconditional love can be healing for mourners.

- Does your grieving friend have a pet? If so, acknowledge the importance of the animal by petting it and talking to it as he does. Perhaps bring the pet an occasional treat.

- If your friend doesn't have a pet, would he like one? Is he a "pet person"? Don't go so far as to buy one for him without his consent because pets are a huge responsibility. And, especially early in grief, most mourners don't have the energy to care for a new pet. But do consider visiting a pet store or your area animal shelter with him.

CARPE DIEM:
Is your friend a dog person? A cat person? A fish person? Buy him a good book on his pet of choice.

GIVE THE GIFT OF SCENT.

- For centuries people have understood that certain smells induce certain feelings. Aromatherapy is the contemporary term for this age-old practice.

- Some comforting, memory-inducing smells include baby powder, freshly cut grass, dill, oranges, leather, lilacs.

- Essential oils, available at your local drugstore or bath and body shop, can be added to bath water or dabbed lightly on pulse points.

- Lavender relaxes. Rosewood and bergamot together lift the spirits. Peppermint invigorates. Chamomile and lavender are sleep aids.

CARPE DIEM:
Visit a local bath and body shop and choose one or two essential oils or scented candles for your friend.

56

CARPE DIEM:
Call your friend
right now and start
making plans for the
overnight.
Brainstorm some
ideas of where to go
and what to do.

PLAN A SLEEPOVER.

- Remember how much fun you had sleeping over at a friend's house when you were a kid? Why not recapture that experience now?

- Slumber parties are chockfull of all the things your grieving friend might need most right now—companionship, laughter, conversation.

- Invite your friend to sleep over at your house this weekend. Make popcorn. Paint your nails. Crawl into sleeping bags in the backyard.

- Or, if that sounds too crazy, plan an overnight getaway with her at a nearby bed and breakfast. Share a room and stay up all night talking. Or go camping and tell stories by the campfire.

GET TO KNOW YOUR SURROUNDINGS.

- Many cities have walking tours of historic or contemporary significant sites—things we often overlook even though they're right under our noses.

- Does your town have a walking tour that you're not aware of? Call your local library or Chamber of Commerce and inquire.

- Are there shops, museums or restaurants in your community that you've never been to before? Invite your friend to visit one with you.

CARPE DIEM:
Call your local extension service and ask for information on native or common trees in your area. Walk through an older section of town with your friend and identify these exquisite giants.

58

STAND IN FOR THE PERSON WHO DIED.

- For your friend, no one can ever take the place of the person who died. But sometimes other people can help with tasks or activities that were the domain of the person who died.

- Did your friend enjoy doing a particular activity with the person who died? Golf? Shopping? Going out to dinner on Tuesdays?

- Did the person who died handle certain chores in the household? Servicing the car? Grocery shopping?

- Offer to stand in for the person who died for a certain task or activity.

CARPE DIEM:
Right now, make a list of the activities your friend used to do with the person who died. If appropriate, also make a list of chores the person who died was responsible for.

IF YOU'RE A MEMBER OF THE MOURNER'S FAMILY, YOU'RE NEEDED THE MOST.

- Family is the cornerstone of most of our lives. With the exception of a few special friends, acquaintances come and go. Family, as they say, is forever.

- Still, in many families, death isn't talked about. It's the elephant in the living room that no one acknowledges.

- You have a special responsibility to the mourner in the weeks and months to come. Be there for your family member. Call her. Visit her. Write her. Spend time with her.

- As a part of this family, you may be grieving the death, as well. You may need to work on meeting your own grief needs before you can help others in your family.

CARPE DIEM:
Consider your family's interpersonal style. Are you close to each other? Only politely friendly? If there are barriers to communication and compassion, maybe you can take the initiative and begin to break them down by helping your grieving family member.

60

IF YOU'RE A MEMBER OF THE MOURNER'S FAMILY, RECOGNIZE THE "PRESSURE COOKER" PHENOMENON.

- If you are among those directly impacted by this death, you and the rest of the family are faced with unique, often all-consuming grief journeys.

- Everyone in the family is stressed by the death; it's a myth to say that "families always get closer at the time of a death."

- Actually, the higher your need to feel understood, the lower your capacity to be understanding for other mourners in the family. And when everyone in the family has a low capacity to be understanding right now, it can feel like a "pressure cooker."

CARPE DIEM:
Give yourself permission to not always "be there" for your family in the coming weeks and months. Renew yourself today. Do something that makes you feel good about life.

IF YOU'RE WORRYING ABOUT SOMETHING, TALK TO YOUR FRIEND.

61

- You're having a party and children will be among those invited but your friend's child has died. Do you invite your friend? Explain your concern to him and let him know you'd like him to come.

- You notice that your friend hardly leaves the house lately and you're concerned. Talk to him.

- You note that your friend is staying very busy—to the point of not being able to mourn. Gently share your observation with him.

- Remember that for supportive confrontation to be helpful, your friend must have the insight to see what you're saying. Some people will welcome your open concern, while others will push you away. Go slow.

CARPE DIEM:
Take inventory of a concern you have for your friend. Think about how you can compassionately and sensitively express this concern to your friend. When the timing seems right, do so.

62

IF THE MOURNER IS A CHILD, THINK LIKE A CHILD.

- Children are often forgotten mourners because adults think they don't feel the loss as deeply or they want to protect them from focusing on the loss.

- Anyone old enough to love is old enough to mourn.

- Remember that children grieve in doses and more through behaviors than through words. But they also need the ongoing presence of loving, supportive adults if they are to heal.

CARPE DIEM:
Take the child to the park and then out for ice cream—just the two of you. Let her know that you're sad about the death, too, and would be happy to talk about it if she'd like to.

SEND ANOTHER CARD. AND ANOTHER.

- Sometimes mourners are overwhelmed at the time of the death by dozens of sympathy cards. Though all are appreciated and healing, those sent later on may have more impact.

- Send a card with a personalized note a month after the death. Send another one a month or two later. Keep sending them in the coming months.

- Don't forget to honor significant dates (such as the birthday of the person who died and the anniversary of the death) with "I'm thinking of you" cards.

CARPE DIEM:
Stop by your local stationers today and select 8-10 blank cards then put them somewhere you won't forget them. Write "send a card to _____" on your planning calendar 5-10 times this year.

64

LISTEN TO THE MUSIC.

- Music can be very healing to mourners because it helps them access their feelings, both happy and sad. Music can soothe the spirit and nurture the heart.

- All types of music can be healing—rock & roll, classical, blues, folk.

- Take your friend to listen to music he normally doesn't, perhaps the opera or the symphony. Or make a recording of your friend's favorite songs all together on one tape.

- Does your friend play an instrument or sing? When you're at his house next, ask him to give you an informal, personal concert.

CARPE DIEM:
Call a nearby elementary school and ask when their next musical program is. Mark it on your calendar and invite your friend along.

DON'T PROSELYTIZE ABOUT YOUR OWN RELIGION.

65

- Your faith may be so strong that you're sure there's life after death and that your friend's loved one is now in paradise. Now is not the time for missionary work. Keep your beliefs to yourself.

- A more appropriate idea is to invite your friend to church or place of worship with you, particularly if she doesn't have a church of her own. If she declines, don't push.

- Faith and mourning are not mutually exclusive. A person can be very faithful yet still mourn.

- Let your friend teach you about her beliefs. Honor them.

CARPE DIEM:
If your friend is a person of faith, write her a supportive note including the words, "Blessed are those who mourn, for they shall be comforted." Let her know you hope to be among those she finds comforting.

66

CARPE DIEM:
Hand-write a coupon for a "pamper day" that entitles your friend to one full day of nurturing. Mail the coupon to him along with a brief note of support.

BE HIS BUTLER FOR A DAY.

- Who wouldn't love to be waited on hand and foot for a day?

- One rainy or snowy day, drop by your friend's house with this mission: to pamper him so he can rest and relax.

- What he's allowed to do: Lounge in bed or on the sofa. Watch TV. Read a book. Talk to you. Call friends long-distance.

- What you'll do for him: Cook. Clean. Serve him lunch on a tray. Play music.

PRAY FOR YOUR FRIEND.

67

- Studies have shown that prayer can actually help people heal.

- If you believe in a higher power, pray for your friend. Pray for her to embrace her pain and to heal over time. Pray for the strength to help her on her journey through grief.

- Many churches have prayer lists. Call your church or your friend's church and ask that her name be added to the prayer list. On Sundays, the whole congregation will pray for her. Often many individuals will pray at home for those on the prayer list, as well.

CARPE DIEM:
Bow your head right now and say a silent prayer for your friend. If you are out of practice, don't worry; just let your thoughts flow naturally.

68

LEAVE YOUR FRIEND ALONE.

- Sometimes the best way to help your grieving friend is to leave him alone.

- Mourning requires a natural turning inward, a contemplative posture of pondering the meaning of life and death.

- Be sure to let your friend know that you'd like to spend some time with him when he's ready. If he rebuffs your invitations, don't be hurt. Instead, offer your presence and support in another week or two.

- Realize that providing your friend with alone time does not mean you are abandoning him.

CARPE DIEM:
Just for today, set aside your worries for your friend. Enjoy *your* life.

GO TO THE WATER.

- Spending time near the ocean, a lake, a river or even a fountain can be restorative. The sound of water is soothing for many people.

- From paddling a canoe to setting sail on a cruise ship, being aboard a waterborne vessel is healing.

- Unless you're sure your friend doesn't get seasick and can swim, don't plan a surprise outing on a boat.

- Many inexpensive tabletop fountains are available at home stores and garden shops today. Buy one for your friend's den or patio.

- Go for a walk in the rain.

CARPE DIEM:
Does a river run through your town? Pack a lunch and invite your friend to picnic with you on the riverbank.

70

CARPE DIEM:
Is your friend over-
whelmed by medical
bills as a result of
this death? Offer to
tie up all the loose
ends by contacting
insurance and health
care providers, etc.
Write up a summary
of the work you've
done so your friend
will have it to refer
to later.

OFFER TO HELP WITH FINANCES.

- Depending on the circumstances of the death, many mourners are confronted with financial loss as well.

- Medical bills, unpaid leaves from work, funeral bills, estate matters, loss of income if the person who died was a breadwinner—all can take their toll on the mourner's sense of stability and can greatly complicate grief.

- Some may need the help of a financial planner to best invest their resources for their future well-being.

- If your friend needs financial help, offer to brainstorm ideas and locate resources for her. Most communities have credit counseling agencies that offer free, sound advice.

LEARN SOMETHING NEW.

- Sometimes mourners feel stuck. They're depressed and the daily routine of their lives is joyless.

- Perhaps your friend would enjoy learning something new or trying a new hobby.

- Are you good at something you could teach your friend? Do you play guitar? Take great photos? Weave baskets?

- Consider physical activities. Learning to play golf or doing karate have the added benefits of exercise.

CARPE DIEM:
With your friend's permission, get ahold of your local community calendar and sign both you and your friend up for a class in something neither of you have ever tried before.

72

TAKE A RISK WITH YOUR FRIEND.

- For some, activities that harbor risk, real or perceived, are invigorating and life-affirming.

- Sometimes people who've encountered death, in particular, feel ready to try limit-stretching activities.

- Some ideas: hang gliding, bungee jumping, skydiving, rock climbing.

- Don't confuse appropriate risk-taking with self-destructiveness. Never encourage your friend to test his own mortality through inappropriate behaviors or inadequate safeguards.

CARPE DIEM:
Schedule a sunrise hot air balloon ride for you and your friend. Toast the dawn with champagne at 5,000 feet.

Picture this.

- The visual arts have a way of making us see the world anew.

- Perhaps your friend would enjoy a visit to an art gallery or museum, a sculpture garden, a photography exhibit.

- Why not try to create some art yourself? Invite your friend to attend a watercolor or calligraphy class.

- Throwing pottery is something almost everyone enjoys. It's tactile and messy and whimsical.

CARPE DIEM:
Buy two disposable cameras—one for you and one for your friend—and take a walk through your friend's neighborhood. Your mission: to capture as many peaceful, joyous images as you can. Have the photos processed at a one-hour lab.

VOLUNTEER ON BEHALF OF YOUR FRIEND.

- Consider honoring the death through social activism. If your friend's loved one was a victim of drunk driving, participate in a local MADD rally. If your friend's baby was stillborn, collect in your neighborhood for The March of Dimes' annual campaign.

- Volunteer at a senior center, an elementary school, a local hospital—someplace befitting the person who died.

- If your schedule is too hectic, offer money instead of time. Make your donation in memory of the person who died. Supportively tell your friend (be humble!) what you've done.

CARPE DIEM:
Call your local United Way and ask for some suggestions about upcoming events you could participate in.

CREATE A CALENDAR.

- A wall calendar commemorating the life of the person who died can be a unique, personalized gift for your friend.

- Use a different photo of the person who died for each month of the year. Type in significant dates to remember on the calender: the birthday of the person who died, your friend's birthday, birthdays of her immediate family, anniversaries, etc.

- Your local copy shop can help you put the calendar together. Or use one of the great computer software packages available today.

CARPE DIEM:
Call your local copy shop and inquire about their capability and process for putting together a personalized calendar.

76

CARPE DIEM:
Watch cartoons with your friend. Looney Tunes are usually good for a laugh, and with Cartoon Network and videos at your local movie store, you should be able to watch them anytime, anywhere.

LAUGH AND YOUR FRIEND MAY LAUGH WITH YOU.

- Humor is one of the most healing gifts of humanity.

- Laughter restores hope and assists in surviving the pain of grief.

- Rent a cornball comedy and invite your friend over for popcorn and a few giggles. Get tickets to a stand-up comedy routine. Watch a slapstick TV show, like The Three Stooges or America's Funniest Home Videos.

VISIT THE GREAT OUTDOORS.

- For many people it is restorative and energizing to spend time outside.

- Mourners often find nature's timeless beauty healing. The sound of a bird singing or the awesome presence of an old tree can help put things in perspective.

- Offer to go on a nature walk with your friend. Or camping. Or canoeing. The farther away from civilization the better.

CARPE DIEM:
Call your area forest service for a map of nearby walking or hiking trails. Then call your friend and schedule a morning hike.

DON'T RELATE STORIES ABOUT SIMILAR DEATHS.

- Remember that this is a unique loss of a unique person. Especially early in your friend's grief, refrain from sharing similar types of stories.

- If your friend's loved one died of breast cancer, for example, refrain from talking about other breast cancer deaths you've heard about—unless your friend asks.

- While it may not be your place to compare deaths, your friend may well find it healing to participate in a support group made up of people who've experienced similar losses.

CARPE DIEM:
Gather information on local support groups that sound appropriate for your friend. Enclose this information in a card along with a supportive note.

HELP YOUR FRIEND MOVE TOWARD HIS GRIEF, NOT AWAY FROM IT.

79

- Our society teaches us that emotional pain is to be avoided, not embraced, yet it is only in moving toward our grief that we can be healed.

- As Helen Keller once said, "The only way to get to the other side is to go through the door."

- Don't ask your friend how he's doing, ask him how he's *surviving*. This question calls for a more honest response.

- As you talk with him, remember this important helping principle: "Enter into what someone thinks and feels without thinking your job is to change what he thinks and feels." In other words, strive for active empathy.

CARPE DIEM:
Write your friend a note reinforcing that you are there to listen to his thoughts and feelings, whatever they may be, and that you will never judge him. Encourage him to talk to you about his grief when he is ready.

80

CARPE DIEM:
Call your local extension office or visit your local library and determine when the next meteor shower will be. Ask your friend to accompany you to a good viewing spot and stay up late watching the show.

CONTEMPLATE THE UNIVERSE.

- Stargazing is a relaxing, renewing activity that's perfect for mourners.

- Do you have a telescope? If so, get it out and refresh your memory on how to use it. If not, gazing at the night sky with the naked eye is just as awe-inspiring.

- Invite your friend for a drive in the country where the city lights won't obscure the starlight. Bring chaise lawn chairs and a couple of blankets so you can lie on your backs and watch in comfort.

- Visit your local planetarium for the next best thing.

HELP YOUR FRIEND SURF THE WEB.

- The World Wide Web has a number of interesting and informative resources for mourners.

- Many articles about grief are available online. Books can also be purchased online. Most grief organizations (The Compassionate Friends, MADD, Widowed Persons Service) now have Web pages.

- Search the word "grief" and see what you find. Use a more specific term (widow, AIDS, etc.) if appropriate.

- Like face-to-face support groups, internet chat groups can be healing for mourners.

CARPE DIEM:
If your friend isn't a computer whiz, offer to sit down with her and do a search. Don't forget to visit the Center for Loss Web site: www.centerforloss.com.

82

CARPE DIEM:
If your friend is being self-destructive, call another trusted friend right now and discuss your concern. Create a plan to supportively confront your friend.

WATCH FOR WARNING SIGNS.

- Sometimes mourners fall back on self-destructive behaviors to get themselves through this difficult time.

- Be aware of drug or alcohol abuse. Talk openly to your friend if you're concerned about such behaviors. Organize an intervention with other friends and family members if you need to.

- Pay attention to suicidal thoughts and feelings. Is your friend isolating himself too much? Is he talking about suicide? Is he giving away possessions? Is he severely depressed?

BRIGHTEN UP YOUR FRIEND'S ENVIRONMENT.

- Would your friend's home or office benefit from a little sprucing up?

- Offer to paint her living room or office in a fresh, new color. Paint is inexpensive and easy to redo.

- Sometimes something as minor as new valances and freshly cleaned windowpanes can make a big difference.

CARPE DIEM:
Buy your friend a new set of sumptuous, all-cotton bed sheets in her favorite color or an appropriate pattern. Don't worry if they don't match her bedroom; no interior decorating rules apply today!

MARK THESE DATES ON YOUR CALENDAR.

- There are at least four critical times to reach out to your grieving friend:

  - immediately after the death
  - two to three weeks after the death
  - six to eight months after the death
  - anniversaries, holidays and other significant events.

- Most mourners are supported at the immediate time of the death but are forgotten later on.

- This is not to suggest that you only contact your friend at these four times; a true companion in grief will be present to his or her friend often in the months and years following the death.

CARPE DIEM:
Get out your calendar and mark these four time periods in bold and all caps. Don't forget!

SIMPLIFY YOUR FRIEND'S LIFE.

- Many of us today are taking stock of what's really important in our lives and trying to discard the rest.

- Mourners are often overwhelmed by all the tasks and commitments they have. If you can help your friend rid himself of some of those extraneous burdens, he'll have more time for mourning and healing.

- What is it that might be overburdening your friend right now? Offer to get him off the junk mail lists, run errands for him, cook a few meals for the freezer.

- Sometimes just helping your friend identify those activities he can give up for now will empower him to do so.

CARPE DIEM:
Mourners often feel obligated to write thank you notes to the many people who sent flowers, food or other gifts at the time of the funeral. Offer to write the notes with him.

86

ESTABLISH A MEMORIAL FUND IN THE NAME OF THE PERSON WHO DIED.

- Sometimes bereaved families ask that memorial contributions be made to specified charities in the name of the person who died. This practice allows friends and family members to show their support while helping the family feel that something good came of the death.

- You can help your friend establish a personalized and ongoing memorial to the person who died.

- What was meaningful to the person who died? Did she support a certain nonprofit or participate in a certain recreational activity? Was she politically active or affected by a certain illness?

- Your local bank or funeral home may have ideas about how to go about setting up a memorial fund.

CARPE DIEM:
Call another friend of the mourner and together brainstorm a list of ideas for a memorial. Suggest that both of you commit to making at least one additional phone call for information before the day is out.

LISTEN TO THE STORY, OVER AND OVER AGAIN IF NECESSARY.

- Acknowledging a death is a painful, ongoing task that's done in doses, over time. A vital part of healing in grief is often "telling the story" over and over again.

- The "story" relates the circumstances surrounding the death, reviewing the relationship, describing aspects of the personality of the person who died, and sharing memories, good and bad.

- It's as if each time the mourner is allowed to tell the story, it becomes a little more real.

- Your friend may want to talk about the death or particular stories of the life over and over again. Try to listen attentively each time.

CARPE DIEM:
Write your friend a note that says something like, "I'm glad you feel like you can talk to me about _____'s death. I'm here for you and I'm ready to listen whenever you'd like."

88

CARPE DIEM:
Call around today
and get a support
group schedule put
together for your
friend. Give it to her
non-confrontationally;
don't insist that she
join a group but
rather suggest that
she might be inter-
ested in one.

INQUIRE ABOUT SUPPORT GROUPS.

- Grief support groups are a healing, safe place for many
  mourners to express their thoughts and feelings.

- Sharing similar experiences with other mourners may help
  your friend feel like she's not alone, that she's not going
  crazy.

- Your local hospice or funeral home may offer a free or
  low-cost support group.

- If your friend is newly bereaved, she may not be ready for a
  support group. Many mourners are more open to joining a
  support group 8-10 months after the death.

TELL YOUR FRIEND HOW IMPORTANT HE IS TO YOU.

- Sometimes mourners feel like their life is no longer worth living after a death. They often are struggling for reasons to get out of bed in the morning.

- Tell your friend how much he matters to you. And tell him why.

- Share the reasons you value your friendship. Tell him about the qualities you admire in him. Remind him how good he is at something he does well.

CARPE DIEM:
Buy a "thinking of you" card and enclose a note that describes the ways in which your friend matters so much to you.

90

PAY ATTENTION TO YOUR NONVERBAL COMMUNICATION.

- At least half of the art of listening and "being there" for your friend involves nonverbal communication.

- Are you looking your friend in the eye when she talks to you? Looking away or distracting yourself with busywork while she's talking communicates that you're either really not listening or uncomfortable with listening.

- Lean into your friend. Nod your head. Keep an open posture. Don't cross your arms in front of your chest.

CARPE DIEM:
Note the nonverbal communication of others today. What can you learn by watching people's bodies and facial expressions as they talk?

DON'T BE OFFENDED IF YOUR FRIEND REBUFFS YOUR ATTEMPTS TO HELP.

- Some mourners feel a stronger need to retreat from support than others.

- Remember—some people, through no fault of their own, never learned that it's OK to need others, thus making it difficult for them to accept your active support. Some will keep you at arm's length.

- Keep in mind that you are responsible to others, not for others.

- Also remember that people are often more receptive to support 8-10 months after a death than they are early in grief.

CARPE DIEM

If your friend rejects your support, don't abandon him. Mark a day two or three weeks from now that you'll try again.

92

CARPE DIEM:
Assemble a "pie kit" for your friend: homemade frozen crust, pie pan, filling, crumb topping, recipe. The smell of fresh pie baking is comforting and irresistible.

MAKE SOMETHING FROM SCRATCH.

- Making something to eat from scratch can be a lot of work, but it can also be a very satisfying and fun activity.

- Baking bread is good therapy. Invite your friend over to bake bread with you one Saturday morning. If neither of you has ever done it before, don't worry! Just follow a recipe.

- Bake a cake from scratch for your friend and deliver it along with a nice note.

VISIT A FARM.

93

- For many people, farms have a wholesome, bucolic, natural feeling that's restorative.

- Sometimes local farms are open to the public. Some dairy farms sell milk or ice cream and many offer tours, for example.

- Many towns have community gardens where you can buy vegetables in season or volunteer. At some fruit farms, you can pick-your-own strawberries or apples.

- Some horse stables rent horses by the day or the hour. Would your friend like to go horseback riding?

CARPE DIEM:
Buy fresh eggs from a local farmer and deliver a dozen to your friend. They're wonderful.

94

HAVE FUN IN THE SUN.

- Take advantage of a nice day by spending it outdoors with your friend.

- Sunshine has a way of making people feel more hopeful about life. In fact, lack of sunshine or daylight has been shown to make people feel depressed.

- Go to the beach, take a walk, have a picnic.

- A sunny day in winter can be enjoyed, too. Go sledding or cross country skiing, ice skate, build a snowman.

CARPE DIEM:
Look out your window. Is it nice out today? Invite your friend on a picnic or to lunch at a restaurant with an outdoor patio.

Take a ride on the Reading.

- Taking a ride just for fun on a passenger train is a relaxing way to spend a day.

- Train rides allow lots of time for conversation and thought.

- You may have an excursion train near you that takes short, scenic trips through the countryside and back again.

- AMTRAK often has affordable fares from city to city or across the country.

CARPE DIEM:
Suggest a train trip to your friend. If she's interested, call your travel agent for more information.

96

REMEMBER YOUR FRIEND DURING THE HOLIDAYS.

- Because the person who died is no longer there to share the holidays with, your friend will probably feel particularly sad and vulnerable during Thanksgiving, Hanukkah or other holidays.

- Invite your friend to share the holidays with you at your house or invite him on a trip during those times.

- Write your friend a note or give him a special gift on each holiday. Make him an ornament at Christmas, dye him a batch of eggs at Easter, take him on a picnic on the 4th of July.

CARPE DIEM:
What's the next major holiday? Plan a way to reach out to your friend on that day.

UNDERSTAND THE CONCEPT OF "RECONCILIATION."

- Sometimes you'll hear about mourners "recovering" from grief. This term is damaging because it implies that grief is an illness that must be cured. It also connotes a return to the way things were before the death.

- Mourners don't recover from grief. They become "reconciled" to it. In other words, they learn to live with it and are forever changed by it.

- This does not mean a life of misery, however. Mourners often not only heal but grow through grief. Their lives can potentially be deeper and more meaningful after the death of someone loved.

- Reconciliation takes time. Your friend may not become truly reconciled to her loss for several years and even then will have "griefbursts" (see Idea 52) forever.

CARPE DIEM:
Keep it in mind in all of your interactions with your friend that she is changed forever by the death. Remember it is not your job to get her "over" grief.

100

CARPE DIEM:
Treat yourself to a lavish bouquet of fresh flowers or that alpaca sweater you've been eyeing. You deserve it. As Eeyore said to Pooh, "You're a real friend."

GIVE YOURSELF A HAND.

- Being a good friend is an art few of us master. Being a good friend to someone in grief is especially hard.

- If you've been there for your grieving friend, if you've been his companion through this most difficult of journeys, you are to be congratulated.

- It is the relationships in our lives that give our lives meaning. You have nurtured a loving relationship as well as helped another human being heal.

- Thank you for your compassion.

CLOSING THOUGHTS

My hope is that this little book has helped you "do something helpful" for a grieving friend. Helping from the heart unfolds when we put aside our own life issues, if only for a moment, and just be there for another person.

If you have been able to achieve this, if you have "companioned" a friend in grief, you are to be congratulated. I thank you for making this world a more compassionate one. And I'm sure your friend thanks you from the bottom of her heart, as well.

To "walk with" our fellow human beings through their struggles is indeed a sacred experience. Trusting in our capacity to heal after the death of someone loved provides us with courage to go to the wilderness of each other's hearts. Yes, hope and trust relate to an orientation of the spirit, an orientation of the heart.

When we truly help from our hearts, we experience a kinship with humanity. When we help from our hearts, we are a part of love in action.

As a family member, friend or caregiver to a person in grief, you are blessed with the opportunity to seize each day. Just as Winnie-the-Pooh so compassionately supported his friend Eeyore, you too have reached out and actively practiced the art of being a "real friend."

Ten Essential Qualities for Family, Friends and Caregivers to the Bereaved

1. Empathy

When you are empathetic, you communicate a real desire to understand and a willingness to be taught about your grieving friend's experience. You don't try to "fix things" but instead are willing to enter into your friend's pain and suffering.

2. Acceptance

To nonjudgmentally allow your grieving friend to share whatever thoughts, feelings and behaviors he needs to is to accept his grief. Acceptance allows for and encourages open mourning and supports the naturalness of the grief response.

3. Sensitivity/Warmth

This quality is primarily communicated nonverbally (smiling, tone of voice, posture, touch) and implies patience and the capacity to hear and respond to your friend's needs.

4. Genuineness

You can help your grieving friend by being yourself, by being sincere in your desire to help. If your friend senses you are genuine she will feel safe in sharing her thoughts and feelings with you.

5. Trust

Trust is about consistency and safety. Can your friend trust you to follow through when you've planned something with him? Does he feel consistently safe and at ease with you?

6. Immediacy

This quality has to do with being present to your friend in the here and now. Are you paying attention to her or are your thoughts elsewhere?

7. Humility

This connotes a willingness to learn from one's own mistakes as well as an appreciation of one's limitations and strengths. Humility also means you are not wiser or the "expert;" your friend is the only expert in his grief.

8. **Patience**

   To be patient with a friend in grief is to let him mourn in his own way and time. You also give him space to think and feel.

9. **Hope**

   It may be impossible to be a real friend in grief without this quality, for it is hope that believes that your grieving friend can and will heal. Hope is an expression of the present alive with a sense of the possible. Hope rallies energies and activates courage to the commitment of mourning.

10. **Heart**

    To have "heart" as you help a friend in grief is to be true to your own feelings, humanness and vulnerabilities. Heart is a metaphor for unconditional love and acceptance of another human being.

SEND US YOUR IDEAS FOR HEALING THE GRIEVING HEART!

My idea:

_____

_____

_____

_____

_____

_____

My name and mailing address:

_____

_____

_____

We'd love to hear your practical ideas for helping a grieving friend. We may use them in future editions of this book or in other publications through the Center for Loss. Please jot down your idea at left and mail it to:

Dr. Alan Wolfelt, The Center for Loss and Life Transition, 3735 Broken Bow Rd. Fort Collins, CO 80526

We look forward to hearing from you!

ALSO BY ALAN WOLFELT

HEALING YOUR GRIEVING HEART
100 PRACTICAL IDEAS

When someone loved dies, we must express our grief if we are to heal. In other words, we must mourn. But knowing *what* to do with your grief and how to mourn doesn't always come naturally. This book offers 100 practical, here-and-now suggestions for helping yourself mourn well so that you may go on to live well and love well again. Turn to any page and seize the day by taking a small step toward healing.

ISBN 1-879651-12-2
128 pages • Softcover • $9.95
(plus additional shipping and handling)

Companion

All Dr. Wolfelt's publications can be ordered by mail from:

Companion Press
3735 Broken Bow Road
Fort Collins, CO 80526

•

(970) 226-6050
Fax 1-800-922-6051

•

All prices are in U.S. dollars and are valid through December, 1998.

THE JOURNEY THROUGH GRIEF: REFLECTIONS ON HEALING

Companion
PRESS

All Dr. Wolfelt's
publications can be
ordered by mail from:

Companion Press
3735 Broken Bow Road
Fort Collins, CO 80526

•

(970) 226-6050
Fax 1-800-922-6051

•

*All prices are in U.S.
dollars and are valid
through December, 1998.*

This spiritual guide to those grieving
the death of someone loved explores the
mourner's journey through grief, in particular
the six needs that all mourners must meet to
heal and grow. Following a short explanation
of each mourning need are a series of short
reflections written to help mourners work on
each need as they feel ready.

Bound in hardcover and designed with grace, *The Journey
Through Grief* is a much-loved, often-referred-to companion on
many mourners' bedside tables.

ISBN 1-879651-11-4
160 pages • Hardcover • $19.95
(plus additional shipping and handling)

UNDERSTANDING GRIEF: HELPING YOURSELF HEAL

A compassionate guide to coping with the death of someone loved, this bestseller helps mourners move toward healing by encouraging them to explore their unique journeys into grief and mourning.

Throughout, readers are asked specific questions about their grief journeys and encouraged to think about and write down their responses. Since its publication in 1992, *Understanding Grief* has been Dr. Wolfelt's most well-known, well-loved book for mourners. Everyone who grieves deserves the support and companionship of this popular, compassionate book.

ISBN 1-55959-038-6
200 pages • Softcover • $19.95
(plus additional shipping and handling)

Companion
PRESS

All Dr. Wolfelt's
publications can be
ordered by mail from:

Companion Press
3735 Broken Bow Road
Fort Collins, CO 80526

•

(970) 226-6050
Fax 1-800-922-6051

•

*All prices are in U.S.
dollars and are valid
through December, 1998.*

THE MOURNER'S BILL OF RIGHTS
A poster & daily affirmation for those who grieve

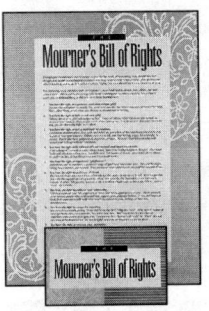

We know that mourners face a difficult journey in our mourning-avoiding culture. This poster helps them remember that each person's grief is unique, and that they have the right to move toward their grief and heal. Sample headings: You have the right to talk about your grief; You have the right to feel a multitude of emotions. A compassionate gift for any grieving person, this poster will fit a standard, ready-made frame. The companion wallet cards, with sturdy laminated covers, fold to credit card size and make tasteful and economical give-aways.

Poster (18" x 24") • $10.00
Wallet cards (packet of 50) • $15.00
(plus additional shipping and handling)